CAT

Douglas Bender

TABLE OF CONTENTS

A Pelican Book

Teaching Tips for Caregivers and Teachers:

Research shows that one of the best ways for students to learn a new topic is to read about it.

Before Reading

- Read the title and predict what the book will be about.
- Read the "Words to Know" and discuss the meaning of each word.
- Read the back cover to see what the book is about.

During Reading

- When a student gets to a word that is unknown, ask them to look at the rest of the sentence to find clues to help with the meaning of the unknown word.
- Motivate students with praise and encouragement.

After Reading

- Discuss the main idea of the book.
- Ask students to give one detail that they learned in the book.

SIGHT WORDS

a
all
black
brown
have
is
jump
like
many
or
play
some
this
to
white
with

WORDS TO KNOW

cat

claws

fur

tails

toys

This is a **cat**.

cat

Many cats have white, black, or brown **fur**.

fur

Some cats have **claws**.

claws

Some cats have **tails**.

tails

All cats like to play with **toys**.

toy

All cats like to jump!

INDEX

Written by: Douglas Bender
Design by: Under the Oaks Media
Series Development: James Earley
Editor: Kim Thompson

Photos: Shutterstock: Africa Studio: cover; 20WZ: p. 5; Edoma: p. 7; Lucky Business: p. 9; Bachkova Natalia: p. 11; absolutimages: p. 13; Krzysztof Smejlis

Library of Congress PCN Data
Cat / Douglas Bender
My First Pet
ISBN 978-1-63897-430-7(hard cover)
ISBN 978-1-63897-545-8(paperback)
ISBN 978-1-63897-660-8(EPUB)
ISBN 978-1-63897-775-9(eBook)
Library of Congress Control Number: 2022932420

Printed in the United States of America.

Seahorse Publishing Company
www.seahorsepub.com

Published in the United States
Seahorse Publishing
PO Box 771325
Coral Springs, FL 33077